# 30 Quick Easy Meals

Perfect for any college student, grad student, or anyone who is limited on time and budget

Rachel Vdolek

# Table of Contents

# Introduction

Since you are reading this, I'm going to guess three things about you:
- You love to eat, but you are sick of takeout
- You want to cook more, but don't have the time or budget
- You need recipes that will come together fast, but won't break the bank

Well, you are in the right place!

This book came about when I was having a conversation with my friend, Ellyn, who is a grad student. She made a suggestion of writing a cookbook for college/grad students who are short on time and budget, because a lot of recipes out there are made for people who have a lot of time. Yes, there are recipes that only take 30 minutes, but what about those that need to have dinner ready in only 20, or even 15, minutes?

Being a college/grad student also typically means that you are only cooking for yourself or maybe one other person (or you end up eating a lot of leftovers!). Most recipes are geared towards the standard 4 person family, so how do you divide 1/4 tsp of something or do you just end up skipping it? And is it worth it to buy a whole container of say, cumin, when you only need a 1/2 tsp?

In this book, you will find those answers, plus lots of tips on how to cook each recipe and how to shop at the grocery store without wasting a lot of food.

I hope this book helps you to cook delicious meals for yourself and maybe inspires you to explore the culinary world a little bit more.

Thanks to Ellyn for all your help! You are awesome!

Rachel

# Tips for cooking

## Shopping Smart:

- Make a list before you go and double check that you have every ingredient you will need for the recipe, including spices.
- If you don't like grocery shopping, make a weekly menu and go only once. Plus, by shopping only once, you are less likely to overspend.
- Don't shop while you are hungry unless you want to spend extra money. Trust me on this one!
- Try to stick to the produce, meat and bulk sections. You should really only need to venture into the inner aisles for staples (spices, sugar, flour, etc.) The less time you spend in the inner aisles, the less likely you are to pick up that extra bag of cookies.
- If your store has a bulk section, take advantage of it! Some recipes only call for a 1/4 c. of nuts, so why buy a whole bag? Plus, bulk is usually cheaper than the bagged stuff in the aisles.
- Same goes for spices! Try to find a store in your area that has a bulk spice section. The prices may scare you off, but trust me, it's cheaper than buying them in the jars (you just need some of your own jars to store it if you buy extra!) And if a recipe calls for only 1/4 tsp, you can buy a 1/4 tsp, usually for just pennies.
- When buying from bulk bins, don't be afraid to take measuring cups with if you aren't good at eyeballing it. It's better to look silly at the store than to not have enough (or waste some) of any ingredient.

## Cooking Smart:

- Read the recipe entirely before you start. If the recipe calls for a diced onion, dice it! It's actually faster to prep everything before you start than to chop as you cook. Plus, you are less likely to forget an ingredient!
- If the recipe you are trying is only one part of the meal, like say a really delicious chicken dish, make the rest of the meal easy. Toss together a simple salad or heat up some frozen veggies. This will cause less stress and save you lots of time.
- Preheat the oven while prepping. Some ovens need 10-15 minutes to reach the desired temperature (even if the dial says its 325F, it may not be!)
- If you a true beginner, I'd suggest following the recipe to a T. Experimenting can be fun, but if it goes awry, it can get really discouraging. Remember, you didn't just magically learn to ride a bike, you started out with training wheels. The recipe is the training wheels! Also, try not to make substitutions unless the recipe says so. Sometimes it may sound good, but until you get the hang of which flavors go with which, it may not be as good as you think.

- Measure everything! Sometimes you may think, oh I'll just eyeball it. It's better to take the time to measure than to accidentally put too much salt or pepper, or heaven forbid, cayenne pepper! Whew that would be spicy!

## Measuring:

- For dry ingredients, use either measuring cups or spoons. For cups, spoon ingredient into cup, the level off with the flat edge of a knife. For spoons, use spoon to take some ingredient out, then, like the cups, level with the flat edge of a knife.
- For wet ingredients, use clear cups with marked lines on the outside, or measuring spoons.
- Always pour ingredients into measuring spoons over another bowl or the sink, not the one you are mixing your ingredients in. I can't tell you how many times I've accidentally poured too much salt and it overflowed into my bowl. Those were some salty cookies!
- Some ingredients have special measuring techniques.
- Brown sugar needs to be compacted to give an accurate measurement. Press down with the back of a spoon to get all the air out when measuring brown sugar.
- Butter usually comes in a wrapper with tbsp measurements on it. Just slice, unwrap and use.
- Flour needs to be stirred before measuring due to the fact that it settles over time and becomes too dense.

# Basic Kitchen Equipment

These are some things everyone should have in their kitchen, no matter what size your kitchen is or how skilled you are.

- Saucepans
    - Good to have at least a 1 quart and a 3 quart for boiling rice and pasta
- Skillets/Sauté pans
    - Best to have at least one 10" and one 12"
    - Nonstick is great for beginning cooks because, well, nothing sticks! But don't buy the cheapest on the market. The better quality one you can afford, the better. It will last you longer and you won't need to buy a new one every few months.
    - If you nonstick pan begins to flake, throw it out and buy a new one!
- Stock pot
    - 5 quart is a good size for making soups, stews and sauces.
- Knives
    - Chef's knife is the most important tool. Be sure to get one that feels comfortable to you and keep it sharp!
    - Paring knife is a smaller sized knife (3-4") and is used for smaller tasks like cutting strawberries or deveining shrimp.
    - Bread knife (serrated) is great to have to slice, well, bread, but using a bread knife for meat and hard to cut winter squashes makes it much easier.
- Cutting boards
    - You need at least one cutting board, two is preferred to keep meat and vegetables separate. I like using wood cutting boards for everything, but I have one polypropylene one (the white kind) that is just for raw meat. Speaking of raw meat....

# Cross Contamination!

- Something every cook should know about, cross contamination happens when you handle raw meat and then handle raw produce or other raw ingredients without washing between. I keep everything separate: separate knives, utensils, cutting boards. If something touches raw meat, I either put it in the sink and get a new one or I wash it thoroughly with hot water and soap before using it again.
- When in doubt, wash your hands! Then again, you should always wash your hands frequently through the cooking process, especially whenever you touch raw meat.
- Keep dish towels and sponges clean. You can kill all the bad bacteria in sponges by throwing them in the microwave for 30 seconds. But be careful! The sponges will get hot!! Let it cool for about 10 minutes before taking it out of the microwave.
- For those plastic polypropylene cutting boards, you can run them through the dishwasher to really disinfect and clean them good. But don't wash your wood boards! They may warp on you and become unusable.
- Keep food in the fridge for no longer than 1 week. Also, don't let food sit out for longer than the time it takes to eat your meal. Ideally, food should be kept below 40 F or above 140 F to prevent spoilage. Refrigerate as soon as you possibly can.
- When in doubt, throw it out! If you aren't sure when you cooked that meal in the back of your fridge, just toss it.
- Place cooked foods on a clean plate. Don't use the same plate you used for the raw meat. And just rinsing doesn't count!
- It is not necessary to wash meat before cooking. In fact, it can actually spread germs and bacteria by splashing the water around.
- To thaw frozen food, let it thaw overnight in the fridge or in the microwave on defrost. Don't let it just sit on the counter during the day. All those bacteria will be itching to get at it since it's at just the right temperature.

Now that's I've told you everything you need to know (well, almost everything), it's time to cook.

Let's eat!

# Soups

Soup is a perfect low budget way to serve dinner. It's also a great way to clean out your fridge or freezer! In fact, some of my best soups have come from using up leftovers.

One of the easiest soups I've made was to take some beef broth and simmer a pack of frozen mixed veggies in it with some chopped onions and garlic, then I added some cubed pieces of leftover steak. Super easy, super quick and you don't waste any good steak!

# Quick Chicken Noodle Soup

20 min cooking time
Serves 2

Who doesn't love chicken noodle soup? I know on a crisp cold day, it's one of my favorite things to eat. But when I get home from a long day I definitely don't feel like making a huge pot of soup that could feed a family of 8 and takes several hours. This version makes just enough for 2 and can be made in under 30 minutes due to the pre-cooked chicken that is simply heated rather than needing to be cooked in the soup. With this recipe, you are ready for any sick day!

1 chicken breast, cooked
1 clove garlic, minced
1 tbsp olive oil
1/4 tsp salt
1/8 tsp pepper
1/2 onion, sliced

1 carrot, sliced
1 stalk celery, sliced
1/2 bag egg noodles
3 cups chicken broth
Parsley, chopped

Shred chicken breast. Heat olive oil in a large soup pot over medium heat. Add veggies and garlic; cook for 3-4 minutes, or until onion is translucent. Add chicken broth and egg noodles.

Bring to a boil, then reduce to simmer; cook for 10 minutes or until noodles are cooked. Add shredded chicken, let simmer for 1 more minute to heat through. Serve with chopped parsley sprinkled over the top.

Calories 412. Total Fat 11.6 g, Sat. Fat 2.1 g, Polyunsat, Fat 1.7 g, Monounsat. Fat 6.5 g. Cholesterol 109.2 mg, Sodium 648.6 mg, Potassium 430.6 mg, Total Carbs 38.3 g, Dietary Fiber 3.3 g, Sugars 4.7 g, Protein 36.0 g

# Chicken and Corn Chowder

30 min cooking time
Serves 2

Chicken and corn chowder is one of my favorite late summer soups. It so flavorful, yet so quick to make, especially if you use pre-cooked chicken. The soup comes together fast, with a simple sauté of the vegetables before adding the stock and chicken. It's so creamy already that you hardly need any additional milk to make it a chowder. Try this soup on a late summer day when you need that extra warmth.

1 chicken breast, cooked and shredded
1/2 yellow onion, diced
1 clove garlic, minced
1/2 green bell pepper, diced
2 c. chicken stock
1/4 tsp salt
1/8 tsp pepper
2 tsp all-purpose flour
1/2 c. milk or alternative milk
1 c. frozen corn

In a large stock pot, heat 1 tbsp oil over medium heat. Add onions, garlic and bell pepper. Sauté for 3-4 minutes until onions begin to soften and turn translucent. Add chicken stock, salt and pepper.

Bring to a boil, then reduce to a simmer and cook for 10 minutes. Meanwhile, mix together flour and milk, then add to pot when simmering is done, along with frozen corn. Cook for 2 minutes until thickened and bubble. Add shredded chicken and cook for 1 more minute until chicken is heated through. Serve hot.

Calories 308. Total Fat 5.1 g, Sat. Fat 1.7 g, Polyunsat, Fat 1.0 g, Monounsat. Fat 1.2 g. Cholesterol 78.1 mg, Sodium 466 mg, Potassium 584 mg, Total Carbs 31.9 g, Dietary Fiber 2.9 g, Sugars 8.5 g, Protein 35.0 g

# Easy Corn and Black Bean Chili for 2 (with leftovers for freezing!)

20 minute prep time plus simmering
Serves 2 plus 2 more servings to put in the freezer

I love vegetarian chilis, especially when they are homemade. They go together so easy and quickly that chilis should definitely be a staple in your home. If you would like to make this a meaty chili, simply brown 1 lb of ground beef or turkey before you cook the onions and garlic. Remove the meat and some of the drippings from the pot while the onions and garlic cook, but add the meat back in when you add the tomatoes. Feel free to change up the beans too! Red kidney beans are a great fit as are pinto beans.

1 yellow onion, diced
2 cloves garlic, minced
1 tbsp oil
3 tomatoes, chopped
1 yellow bell pepper, chopped
1/2 c. water

1 tsp each cumin and chili powder
1/4 tsp salt
1/8 tsp pepper
14 oz can black beans, drained and rinsed
1 c. frozen corn

In a large pot or Dutch oven, heat oil over medium heat. Add onions and garlic and sauté for 3-4 minutes. Add tomatoes and bell peppers and sauté for 3-4 minutes.

Add water and seasonings, and let simmer for 10-30 minutes, depending on how much time you have. The longer you let it simmer, the better it will taste. Just before serving, add in black beans and corn. Let simmer for 5 minutes to heat corn and beans.

Calories 189. Total Fat 4.6 g, Sat. Fat 0.6 g, Polyunsat, Fat 0.6 g, Monounsat. Fat 2.7 g. Cholesterol 0 mg, Sodium 521.6 mg, Potassium 351.1 mg, Total Carbs 35.9 g, Dietary Fiber 7.4 g, Sugars 3.6 g, Protein 8.0 g

# Kale and Tomato Soup with White Beans
30 minute cooking time
Serves 2

Eating kale in soup is my favorite way to get more greens in my diet. If kale is a bit on the wild side for you, feel free to substitute any leafy green, such as spinach or chard. If tomatoes are not available in your area or it's the dead of winter, feel free to substitute 1 can of diced tomatoes with juices. I enjoy the fire roasted kind that add an extra smokiness. For a bit of meatiness, I sometimes sauté some chopped up bacon with the onions and garlic. This soup is so forgiving and can be modified for any taste. Even my meat loving brother said it was pretty good for hippie soup!

1 tbsp oil
1/2 yellow onion, diced
1 clove garlic, minced
3 tomatoes, chopped
2 c. chicken or vegetable stock

1 tsp Italian seasoning blend
1/4 tsp salt
1/8 tsp pepper
1 bunch kale, chopped
1 can white beans, drained and rinsed

In a large stock pot, heat oil over medium heat. Add onions and garlic and sauté for 3-4 minutes until onion becomes translucent. Add chopped tomatoes with juices and sauté for 3 more minutes.

Add stock and seasonings, bring to a boil, then reduce heat to low to simmer for 10 minutes. Add kale and beans, continuing to cook over low heat for another 3-4 minutes until kale is wilted and beans are heated.

Serve with some fresh bread.

Calories 379.1. Total Fat 8.2 g, Sat. Fat 1.2 g, Polyunsat, Fat 1.2 g, Monounsat. Fat 5.1 g. Cholesterol 0 mg, Sodium 410.6 mg, Potassium 1402.7 mg, Total Carbs 60.1 g, Dietary Fiber 13.1 g, Sugars 3.4 g, Protein 20.1 g

# Tortilla Soup

20 minutes cooking time
Serves 2

Tortilla soup is a favorite at my place. I never had a really good tortilla soup until I went to Mexico (duh!) but I swear this one comes close. It requires just a little simmering to mix the flavors together, and tastes even better the next day. This soup always cures my craving for tortilla soup and is much easier on the wallet than going out.

1/2 yellow onion, diced
1 clove garlic, minced
1 tbsp oil
14 oz can diced tomatoes
2 1/4 c. chicken stock
1 tsp taco seasoning
1/4 tsp salt
1/8 tsp pepper
1 tsp to 1 tbsp Mexican hot sauce
1 avocado, diced
Tortilla chips

In a large stock pot, heat oil over medium heat. Add onion and garlic and sauté for 3-4 minutes until onion becomes translucent. Pour tomatoes with juices into a blender, then add onions and garlic plus 1/4 c. stock.

Puree until smooth, then pour into stock pot. Heat tomato mixture over medium heat for 2 minutes, then add stock, taco seasoning, salt and pepper. Bring to a boil, then simmer over low for 6-8 minutes. Stir in hot sauce, if desired, for additional spiciness. To serve, ladle into bowls and top each with some diced avocado and some crumbled tortilla chips.

Calories 179.1. Total Fat 9.9 g, Sat. Fat 1.1 g, Polyunsat, Fat 0.7 g, Monounsat. Fat 5.5 g. Cholesterol 0 mg, Sodium 850.0 mg, Potassium 399.7 mg, Total Carbs 15.9 g, Dietary Fiber 2.3 g, Sugars 6.3 g, Protein 5.1 g

# Salads

Big salads are great. I eat a nice big veggie filled salad at least twice a week, if not more often. I love coming up with new combinations at the salad bar, especially when they rotate in new foods.

If you can, I highly suggest finding a grocery store near you that has a salad bar, even if it's tiny. To be able to buy only enough pre-chopped lettuce for one salad versus buying a huge bag that may go to waste is a huge money saver. Unless of course you eat a lot of salad in a week, then by all means, buy the big bag!

# Tuna and Chickpea Salad

10 minute prep time
Serves 2

This was my go-to salad when I didn't bring anything to work. I would go to my grocery store that had a salad bar and get a little bit of everything, then top it with a can of tuna and dress it in a balsamic vinaigrette. If your grocery store has a salad bar, simply pick up the pre-cut veggies and then mix together at home. Feel free to substitute any bean or any veggie you like.

1 can tuna, preferably oil packed, slightly drained
1 can chickpeas, drained and rinsed
¼ onion, sliced thinly or about 5 slices of onion
½ cucumber, sliced or about 10 slices
½ bell pepper, chopped, or about 1 c. chopped
Handful cherry tomatoes, halved
2 tbsp. balsamic vinegar
1/4 c. olive oil
Salt and pepper

Mix together balsamic vinegar and olive oil for dressing. Combine the rest of ingredients and toss with dressing.

Calories 661.8. Total Fat 36.4 g, Sat. Fat 5.2 g, Polyunsat, Fat 5.8 g, Monounsat. Fat 22.9 g. Cholesterol 15.4 mg, Sodium 594.3 mg, Potassium 754.4 mg, Total Carbs 49.7 g, Dietary Fiber 9.5 g, Sugars 0.6 g, Protein 35.1 g

# Steak and Corn Salad

Makes 2 salads

30 min cooking time

This salad is great because you can make enough for dinner tonight and lunch tomorrow. It packs very well as long as you keep everything separate until you are ready to eat. Just heat the steak in the microwave for 30 seconds, then toss everything together. Yum!

1 sirloin steak, about 1/2 lb

1/4 tsp each coriander, chili powder, cumin, paprika, salt, pepper

1 c. corn, thawed if frozen

1/4 c. halved grape tomatoes

Your favorite greens

Dressing:

Juice of 1/2 lime

1/4 c. olive oil

1/2 tsp sugar

1/4 tsp Mexican hot sauce

1 small handful cilantro, chopped

1/4 tsp salt

1/8 tsp pepper

In a medium bowl, combine all ingredients for the dressing. Add corn and tomato halves, and set aside to marinate. For the steak, mix together spices, then rub the steak. Let stand for 10 minutes, then grill over medium-high heat until medium rare, flipping once. Remove from pan and let rest for 10 minutes. Slice thinly.

Put a few handfuls of lettuce into each bowl, then top with some steak slices and a spoonful or two of the corn mixture.

Calories 581.8. Total Fat 44.9 g, Sat. Fat 10.2 g, Polyunsat, Fat 2.7 g, Monounsat. Fat 20.2 g. Cholesterol 76.0 mg, Sodium 548.4 mg, Potassium 339.7 mg, Total Carbs 24.1 g, Dietary Fiber 3.8 g, Sugars 4.4 g, Protein 26.1 g

# Spicy Shrimp Salad

Makes 2 salads

15 minute cooking time

I love this super simple salad. The part that takes the longest is cooking the shrimp. Everything else is simply dice, mix and toss. How great is that? This salad also does well packed for lunch the next day.

10 shrimp, peeled and deveined

1/4 tsp cayenne (or more if you like it spicy)

1/2 tsp ground cumin

1 tsp grated fresh ginger

2 green onions, sliced on bias

2 tbsp lime juice

4 tbsp olive oil

Cilantro, chopped

Avocado, diced

Arugula or your favorite greens

Heat a sauté pan over medium high heat. Add 1 tbsp olive oil and cook shrimp until curled, and just barely pink. Set aside to cool slightly.

Mix together cayenne, cumin, ginger, green onions, lime juice and olive oil to make the dressing. Add shrimp and toss to coat. Add in cilantro and diced avocado; then toss. Serve over a bed of arugula.

Calories 336.8. Total Fat 32.1 g, Sat. Fat 3.8g, Polyunsat, Fat 2.5 g, Monounsat. Fat 20 g. Cholesterol 45.6 mg, Sodium 66.6 mg, Potassium 229.4 mg, Total Carbs 6.8 g, Dietary Fiber 2.2 g, Sugars 0.8 g, Protein 7.8g

# Smoked Salmon, Asparagus and Avocado Salad

Makes 2 salads
20 min cooking time

I just love this salad. I have been making it since my first year of college where I used my microwave steamer to cook the asparagus. Since then, I've upgraded to using boiling water to cook the asparagus, but the flavor is still the same. If you can't find or don't want to splurge on raspberry vinegar, just take a few thawed frozen raspberries and mash them into 1 tbsp of vinegar to get the same flavor.

1 bunch asparagus, trimmed and cut in half
1/2 lb fillet of smoked salmon
1 avocado
feta cheese or baby mozzarella
lettuce greens

Dressing:
1 tbsp raspberry vinegar
1/4 tsp lemon zest
3 tbsp olive oil
1/4 tsp salt and 1/8 tsp pepper

Bring a pot of water to a boil, then add asparagus. Cook for 2 minutes or until emerald green in color and just tender enough a fork can spear them. Drain and set aside to cool.

Flake salmon fillet, removing any bones and skin. Cut the avocado into slices. Whisk together ingredients for the dressing.

To assemble salad, layer lettuce greens on each plate, then top with flaked salmon, half of the asparagus spears, avocado slices and sprinkle crumbled cheese over the top. Drizzle with dressing and serve.

Calories 461.9. Total Fat 35.8 g, Sat. Fat 8.6 g, Polyunsat, Fat 3.6 g, Monounsat. Fat 21.5 g. Cholesterol 51.3 mg, Sodium 2895.1 mg, Potassium 533.8 mg, Total Carbs 8.5 g, Dietary Fiber 2.9 g, Sugars 0.5 g, Protein 27.7 g

# Homemade Small Batch Dressings (Ranch, Honey Mustard, Balsamic, Italian)

10 minutes prep time
Makes enough for 1-2 salads

I love making my own salad dressings at home to save money and calories, but most of the time I end up wasting a ton of it when I make a huge batch. But no longer! These small batch dressings with save you tons of money because you won't be wasting any and since they are freshly made, they will taste better than any store bought dressing. Each batch makes enough for 1-2 salads depending on how much dressing you like to drizzle over your greens.

Ranch:

1 tbsp mayonnaise
1 1/2 tbsp milk
1/8 tsp parsley
1/8 tsp dill
1/8 tsp garlic salt

Balsamic:

1 tbsp balsamic vinegar
3 tbsp olive oil
1/8 tsp dry mustard

Honey Mustard:

1 tbsp mustard
1 tbsp olive oil
1 tbsp white wine vinegar
1 tbsp honey

Italian:

3 tbsp olive oil
1 tbsp white wine vinegar
1/4 tsp Italian herb mix
1/8 tsp garlic salt

To make, mix all ingredient together in a bowl then whisk to combine. The Italian and Balsamic dressings may separate and will need a little more whisking before serving.

The picture shows the Italian dressing on a salad of cucumber slices cubed radish, peas, smoked salmon and parsley. .

# Sandwiches

I am always searching for new sandwich ideas, especially if they carry well for hiking or skiing. Even when I'm not out going on an adventure, I still love making sandwiches at home. They are so easy to prepare and they are delicious!

When making a sandwich, the sky is the limit. There are so many different combinations that I can't even start to count. Some of my favorite easy sandwiches include:

-Roast beef with greens and red pepper pesto (and maybe a bit of goat cheese or mozzarella)
-Ham with mustard and pickles
-Sliced turkey with herbed mustard and roasted red bell peppers

# Garlic Shrimp Roll with Coleslaw

Makes 2 sandwiches
20 min cooking time

This sandwich is one of my favorites to make. It goes together quickly and disappears even quicker. To up the healthy factor, feel free to substitute whole wheat buns and to up the coleslaw amount.

8 shrimp, peeled and deveined
2 tbsp butter
2 cloves garlic, minced
1/4 tsp salt
1/4 tsp pepper
1/2 bag coleslaw veggie mix
1 tbsp mayo
1 tbsp olive oil
1 tsp white wine vinegar
1/4 tsp salt
1/4 tsp sugar

2 hoagie rolls or hot dog buns

Mix together mayo, oil, vinegar, salt and sugar. Add to coleslaw mix and toss to combine. Set aside.

Heat a medium sauté pan over medium high heat. Add butter. When melted, add garlic and cook for 30 seconds, then add shrimp, salt and pepper. Cook until pink and curled up, about 3-4 minutes, stirring to prevent sticking. Serve 4 shrimp each on a hoagie roll and top with coleslaw, if desired.

Calories 362.9. Total Fat 25.1 g, Sat. Fat 9.3 g, Polyunsat, Fat 1.8 g, Monounsat. Fat 8.8 g. Cholesterol 54.4 mg, Sodium 878.6 mg, Potassium 99.6 mg, Total Carbs 27.7 g, Dietary Fiber 3.0 g, Sugars 5.8 g, Protein 7.9 g

# Sweet Pepper and Salami Panini

Makes 2 sandwiches
15 minute cooking time

I love paninis, especially this one. It's got peppers and onions, which I love to eat on everything, and then adds in some good salami for a hint of saltiness. A dollop of mayo on the bread makes it all stick together before being squished into deliciousness. If you would prefer, feel free to use thin sliced turkey instead of the salami.

1 red bell pepper, cut into strips
1/2 yellow onion, cut into slices
1 clove garlic, minced
1 tbsp mayo
2 oz salami, about 10 slices
2 ciabatta rolls or 2 slices of bread

In a large sauté pan over medium high heat, cook peppers, onions and garlic in 1 tbsp oil for 5-7 minutes or until crisp tender and onions begin to caramelize. If you like your onions a bit more cooked, continue cooking them to your liking. They won't cook much more once in the sandwich, so be sure to cook em good!

To assemble sandwiches, cut ciabattas in half, is using. Spread half the mayo on one side of each pair of bread halves, then top each with 5 slices of salami (or more if desired). Add peppers and onions on top, then top with other half of bread. Press in a panini press for 3-4 minutes on each side, or if you don't have a panini press, heat a sauté pan over medium heat, then place sandwich in pan and top with another pan. Press down for 3-4 minutes, then flip sandwich over and repeat. Cut sandwich in half diagonally and serve hot.

Calories 598. Total Fat 25.7g, Sat. Fat 5.7 g, Polyunsat, Fat 1.6 g, Monounsat. Fat 9.8 g. Cholesterol 24.2 mg, Sodium 1465 mg, Potassium 286.5 mg, Total Carbs 76.9 g, Dietary Fiber 4.2 g, Sugars 6.7 g, Protein 18.7 g

# Veggie Sandwich with Hummus

Makes 1 sandwich

10 min prep time

This sandwich came about when I was stuck at the store and needed something quick and healthy for lunch, but I didn't feel like having a salad. I had bread at home and some hummus, so I decided to try some hummus on the bread with a few veggies. I was surprised at how good it was! The great part about this sandwich is that you can get whatever veggies you feel like and so it's easily customizable. Plus, you can switch up the regular hummus to my favorite, roasted red pepper hummus, for an extra dose of flavor.

2 slices of your favorite bread

1-2 tbsp hummus

1 c. veggies from salad bar

Spread hummus on one slice of bread, then top with veggies. Place other slice of bread on top and devour.

*Some of my favorite combos:

-baby kale, tomatoes, onions, bell pepper and pepperoncini

-spring mix, peas, onions, bell peppers, shredded carrots

-romaine, chicken, parmesan, tomatoes, onions

For hummus and bread plus 1 c. greens: Calories 305.0. Total Fat 10 g, Sat. Fat 1.0 g, Polyunsat, Fat 0 g, Monounsat. Fat 0g. Cholesterol 0 mg, Sodium 450 mg, Potassium 240 mg, Total Carbs 45 g, Dietary Fiber 14 g, Sugars 8 g, Protein 15 g

# Hoisin Chicken Lettuce Wraps

Serves 2 plus leftovers that make a great salad

30 min cooking time

My mom loves lettuce wraps and has this favorite one from a local restaurant. I haven't been able to duplicate theirs, but this one comes close. If you don't like water chestnuts, you can always crumble up some dry ramen noodles and sprinkle them on top for some crunch.

1 lb ground chicken
½ onion, diced
2 garlic cloves, minced
1 can water chestnuts, drained and chopped
¼ c. soy sauce
¼ c. hoisin
1 tbsp sesame oil
2 green onions, sliced
Red leaf lettuce, rinsed, leaves separated individually

In a large sauté pan, heat 1 tbsp olive oil over medium-high heat. Add onions and garlic, and sauté for 2 minutes until onion begins to get translucent. Add chicken and brown, about 4-5 minutes, stirring occasionally until no more pink remains.

Add water chestnuts, soy sauce, hoisin, sesame oil, and green onions. Stir to combine.

To serve, pour chicken mixture into a large bowl and let people grab their own lettuce leaves and spoon the chicken mixture into the leaves. Roll up the leaves and devour.

Calories 298.3. Total Fat 15.3 g, Sat. Fat 4.0 g, Polyunsat, Fat 1.7 g, Monounsat. Fat 1.5 g. Cholesterol 84.9 mg, Sodium 1259.4 mg, Potassium 288.4 mg, Total Carbs 18.6 g, Dietary Fiber 2.3 g, Sugars 3.8 g, Protein 22.8 g

# French Dip

30 min cooking time
Makes 2 sandwiches

French dip sandwiches were always one of my favorite sandwiches growing up. There's something so comforting about roast beef on a roll with some delicious juices to dip it in. Just thinking about it is making me hungry! This recipe is a little different than your traditional French dip in that the roast beef is pre-sliced from the deli and is just slightly simmered in some herby onion beef broth before being loaded up on a roll, and so it takes fractions of the time compared to cook a whole roast and slicing it yourself.

1/2 yellow onion, sliced
1 clove garlic, minced
1 tsp oil
2 c. beef stock
1/4 tsp rosemary
1/8 tsp pepper
1/2 lb sliced deli roast beef
2 ciabatta buns or hoagie rolls

In a medium sauce pan, heat oil over medium high heat. Add onions and garlic and sauté for 3-4 minute or until onions become tender. Add stock, rosemary and pepper. Bring to a boil, then reduce heat to low and simmer for 10 minutes. Add beef slices and cook for another 5 minutes.

Split ciabatta or hoagie rolls in half lengthwise. Layer half of the beef on each roll and top with onions. Put other half of roll on top, and cut in half on a bias. Pour broth into 2 bowls and serve with each sandwich.

Calories 600.5. Total Fat 11.6 g, Sat. Fat 2.7 g, Polyunsat, Fat 0.4 g, Monounsat. Fat 3.6 g. Cholesterol 51.5 mg, Sodium 3103.0 mg, Potassium 497.2 mg, Total Carbs 79 g, Dietary Fiber 2.7 g, Sugars 4.3 g, Protein 46.3 g

# On the Stove, In the Oven

This section is all about easy cooking that takes just a few minutes of prep time but requires some hands-off cooking. I love doing this kind of cooking when I get home a little early but have a million other things to and can't sit at the stove for an hour.

Some of these recipes do require making sides to go with the main meal, such as the chicken teriyaki. But don't fear! I've included many easy sides that can be prepared in minutes while everything is cooking. Try some of these recipes on a weekend at home when there is laundry to be done because all of these will make your home smell delicious!

# Grilled Teriyaki Chicken

30 min cooking time
Serves 2

Chicken teriyaki was one of my favorite takeout meals in college. I swear I would eat it at least twice a week if not more. But every time I ate out, it would be up to $8 a plate. By making it at home, you save money and you can create a flavorful meal that is lower in sodium and other preservatives. My favorite way to serve this is to throw some brown rice in a rice cooker before I even start the chicken and then while the chicken is baking I cook some mixed veggies in the microwave. It makes for a meal that is just as quick as driving to get takeout.

4 boneless skinless chicken thighs, cut into strips if you would like to save time

Marinade:
2 tbsp soy sauce
2 tbsp mirin (sweet rice wine)
2 tbsp sesame oil
1 tsp honey or sugar

In a medium bowl, mix together ingredients for marinade, then add chicken. Let sit for 10 minutes to marinate. Heat up a skillet or grill pan over medium high heat. Add chicken to pan. If using strips, continually stir until cooked. If using whole thighs, flip once after about 5 minutes of grilling and continue to grill for another 4 minutes or until chicken registers 160 F on a thermometer.

For chicken only: Calories 328.5. Total Fat 19.0 g, Sat. Fat 3.3 g, Polyunsat, Fat 7.0 g, Monounsat. Fat 7.1 g. Cholesterol 114.5 mg, Sodium 1150.7 mg, Potassium 355.3 mg, Total Carbs 11.1 g, Dietary Fiber 0.1 g, Sugars 7.1g, Protein 28.1 g

# Baked Lemon Rosemary Chicken with Broccoli and Rice

10 min prep time
Serves 2 with enough for leftovers

This recipe is a hit for weeknights when you want something quick but comforting. The chicken is baked in a hotter oven for a faster cooking time, but still remains juicy and delicious. I suggest microwaving or steaming some broccoli to go with the chicken because it's something you can easily prepare while the chicken is baking. As for the rice, you can buy some pre-cooked rice at any store with a Chinese deli, or I highly suggest investing in a rice cooker. It will save you time and money, and always give you perfectly cooked rice. For 4 servings, you will need 1 c. rice and 2 c. water for the rice cooker. Easy as pie!

4 chicken thighs, bone-in, skin on
1 lemon, sliced
1 sprig rosemary
Salt and pepper
Olive oil

Frozen broccoli, thawed and cooked as desired
Rice, cooked as desired

Preheat oven to 400 F. Lay chicken thighs in a medium ceramic or glass baking dish. Using your finger, separate the skin from the meat without tearing it completely off. You want to create a pocket, essentially, and then stuff 1 lemon slice and a few blades of rosemary under the skin of each thigh. Sprinkle salt and pepper over the top of each, then drizzle with oil, being sure to coat the top and bottom of the thighs.

Bake thighs for 15-20 minutes or until a thermometer reads 160 F and the skin is crispy. Remove pan from oven and cover with foil. Let rest 5 minutes for the juices to redistribute, then serve with rice and broccoli.

For chicken only: Calories 224.2. Total Fat 12.2 g, Sat. Fat 2.3 g, Polyunsat, Fat 1.9 g, Monounsat. Fat 6.6 g. Cholesterol 114.5 mg, Sodium 196.3 mg, Potassium 320.6 mg, Total Carbs 0.1 g, Dietary Fiber 0.0 g, Sugars 0 g, Protein 27.1 g

# Beef Stroganoff

Serves 2
30 minute cooking time

I grew up on beef stroganoff. My mom made it so often that I absolutely love it. What I don't love is the long simmering. Who has time to simmer beef chuck until it's soft and tender? On a weeknight, I sure don't! I came up with a solution: use steak cuts instead! The price is a bit higher, but it makes up for it in its ease to cook. I also have upped the amount of mushrooms typically used in this dish to add meatiness without making it expensive by adding more meat.

3/4 lb sirloin steak, cut into 1" cubes
1 tbsp oil
1/2 lb cremini mushrooms or button mushrooms, sliced
1/2 yellow onion, diced
1 clove garlic, minced

1 c. beef stock
1/4 tsp Worcestershire sauce
1 tsp Dijon or herbed mustard
Sour cream or crème fraiche, optional
1 c. egg noodles or fusilli

Bring a large pot of water to a boil, then cook noodles according to package directions. Drain and set aside.

In a large sauté pan, heat 1 tbsp oil over medium high heat. Add steak cubes and sear on 2 opposite sides, turning once, cooking for about 2-3 minutes per side. The steak will still be very raw inside, but it will be cooked more later in the sauce. Remove steak from pan and set aside on a plate. Add a little more oil if necessary, then add mushrooms, onions and garlic. Sauté for 3-4 minutes until onions are beginning to brown and mushrooms are becoming soft.

Add stock and Worcestershire sauce to pan and bring to a boil. Reduce to simmer over low heat and cook for 10 minutes, or until sauce is reduced by about half. Stir in mustard, then add steak back into pan, along with any accumulated juices. Stir in a large dollop of sour cream, if desired. Serve over noodles.

Without sour cream: Calories 549.5. Total Fat 33.3 g, Sat. Fat 10.7 g, Polyunsat, Fat 0.8 g, Monounsat. Fat 5.2 g. Cholesterol 134.6 mg, Sodium 453.4 mg, Potassium 554.5 mg, Total Carbs 23.0 g, Dietary Fiber 1.6 g, Sugars 3.7 g, Protein 43.7 g

# Beef Tacos

Serves 2

30 minute cooking time

I love making tacos. Taco night was one of my favorites growing up, and I continue that tradition by experimenting with different veggies and meats. This recipe is one of my easiest and quickest ones that has tons of flavor but can be made super quickly. If you don't have time to make the guacamole, store bought will do in a pinch.

1/2 lb ground beef

1/2 sweet onion, finely chopped

1 clove garlic, minced

1 tbsp olive oil

1 tsp chili powder

1 tsp cumin

1/2 tsp coriander

1/4 tsp cayenne

1/4 tsp salt and 1/8 tsp pepper

Guacamole:

1 large avocado

2 vine-ripened tomatoes, chopped, 1/4 reserved for topping

1 handful cilantro, chopped

1/2 lime, juiced

1/4 tsp salt

1/8 tsp pepper

Lettuce leaves, chopped

Lime wedges

Yellow corn tortillas

Heat oil in a large sauté pan over medium heat. Cook until garlic begins to brown, about 30 seconds, then add onions. Cook onions for 4-5 minutes, until translucent. Remove from pan and set aside. Cook beef until there is no more pink visible. Stir in spices and onion mixture, and set aside. To make guacamole, mash avocado in a bowl. Stir in lime juice, tomatoes, salt, pepper and cilantro. To serve: heat tortillas over medium heat in a nonstick sauté pan. Top with beef mixture, guacamole, lettuce, diced tomato and sprinkle with lime juice.

With guacamole: Calories 747.5. Total Fat 46.5 g, Sat. Fat 11.9 g, Polyunsat, Fat 4.3 g, Monounsat. Fat 24.5 g. Cholesterol 85.1 mg, Sodium 687.2 mg, Potassium 958.4 mg, Total Carbs 62.1 g, Dietary Fiber 11.3 g, Sugars 1.6 g, Protein 28.6 g

# Paprika Chicken with Potatoes

Serves 2

10 minutes active time, 45 minutes cooking time

The version of this dish that I grew up eating is called
Chicken Paprika and it's a Czech/Hungarian dish that
requires a long simmering time in a heavy sour cream
based sauce. While it's very delicious, it's not exactly
the healthiest, especially when you serve it with super
dense salty dumplings! This is my quicker and
healthier version, which is baked rather than
simmered, and is served with crispy potatoes rather
than dumplings. Serve with some mixed veggies heated
in the microwave or a nice green salad and you will get
a taste of Czech cuisine.

2 chicken thighs

2 potatoes, quartered

1 cloves garlic, minced

2 tbsp paprika

1/4 tsp Salt and 1/8 tsp pepper

Juice from ½ lemon

Olive oil

Preheat oven to 425F. Place chicken thighs in a roasting dish and surround with
potatoes. Sprinkle minced garlic over the top. Dust potatoes and chicken with paprika,
salt and pepper. Drizzle with lemon juice and olive oil. Toss to coat. Bake for 30 minutes
or until thighs are done (register 160F on thermometer). The potatoes may need an extra
5-10 minutes to get extra crispy. Serve with green salad.

Salad not included: Calories 277.2. Total Fat 10.4 g, Sat. Fat 1.7 g, Polyunsat, Fat 1.8 g, Monounsat. Fat 5.9 g.
Cholesterol 57.3 mg, Sodium 352.8 mg, Potassium 963.4 mg, Total Carbs 31.4 g, Dietary Fiber 4.7 g, Sugars 2.0 g,
Protein 17.7 g

# Pasta

Pasta pasta pasta! I love pasta! And noodles. And everything you can consider a pasta or a noodle. But what I don't love is that many recipes call for slathering it in a heavy cream based sauce. I prefer to eat my pasta a little more naked thank you! You will find many of my recipes are a bit light on the sauces because I like less sauce on my pasta, but if you like them a bit saucier, you can always add more sauce.

# Asian Noodle Veggie Stir Fry

Serves 2
20 minute cooking time

Here is another easy meal from the salad bar. I love that I can just crab an assortment of veggies and mix it with some noodles, then stir fry them into deliciousness. I added chicken to the one in the picture, but feel free to add any meat you would like, or just leave it veggie-full!

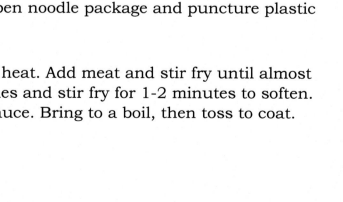

Pre-cut veggies from the salad bar, your choice (at least 2 c.)
1/2 lb skirt steak, chicken breasts or shrimp
1 package yakisoba noodles

Sauce:
3 tbsp soy sauce
1 tbsp rice vinegar
½ tbsp sesame oil
½ tbsp mirin (rice wine)
1 tbsp hoisin
¼ tsp Sriracha, optional

For meat, slice steak into thin slices, cut chicken into 1" cubes, or peel and devein shrimp.

Mix together ingredients for sauce. Set aside. Open noodle package and puncture plastic with scissors. Put in microwave for 30 seconds.

Heat a large non-stick sauté pan over med-high heat. Add meat and stir fry until almost done. Remove from pan and set aside. Add veggies and stir fry for 1-2 minutes to soften. Add meat and noodles back into pan and add sauce. Bring to a boil, then toss to coat.

With chicken: Calories 376. Total Fat 5.4 g, Sat. Fat 1.0 g, Polyunsat, Fat 1.1 g, Monounsat. Fat 1.1 g. Cholesterol 73.4 mg, Sodium 1652 mg, Potassium 583.7 mg, Total Carbs 46.3 g, Dietary Fiber 6.6 g, Sugars 2.1 g, Protein 35.8 g

# Tuna Alfredo with Peas

Serves 4

20 minute cook time

My grandma did not like to cook, but she had to confront this necessary evil in order to feed her grandkids when we were on camping trips. One of the meals she fed us was a tuna alfredo boxed pasta that I loved to add peas to. This recipe is my healthier versions of that boxed pasta, with the peas added in of course!

1 can tuna, drained

1 c. frozen peas

1 clove garlic minced

1/2 c. crème fraiche or Greek yogurt

1/4 c. heavy cream

1/2 lb fettuccine

Grated Parmesan cheese

Bring water in a large stockpot to a boil, then cook fettuccine according to package directions. Drain and set aside.

Cook garlic in 1 tbsp butter until lightly browned. Add tuna, peas, crème fraiche or yogurt, cream and fettuccine. Let gently simmer for 2-3 min until thickened and peas are warmed. Add water to thin sauce if desired. Sprinkle with Parmesan cheese.

With yogurt: Calories 668.2. Total Fat 14.9 g, Sat. Fat 8.0 g, Polyunsat, Fat 0.8 g, Monounsat. Fat 3.4 g. Cholesterol 71.8 mg, Sodium 362.5 mg, Potassium 363.4 mg, Total Carbs 97.3 g, Dietary Fiber 7.1 g, Sugars 7.9 g, Protein 40.5 g

# Bowties with Broccolini and Sausage (or Beans)

Serves 4

20 minute cook time

I came up with this meal a few years ago when I was trying to figure out a way to cook some broccolini that I bought. What is broccolini you ask? It's like broccoli but with longer stalks that aren't as fibery and chewy. It has the same great taste as broccoli, but I like it way more! If you can't find broccolini, regular broccoli florets will substitute just fine.

1 lb. broccolini, ends trimmed and roughly chopped

1 tbsp olive oil, plus more for sprinkling

1 lb chicken Italian sausage, casings removed and sliced or crumbled (or 16 oz. can white beans, drained and rinsed)

2 garlic cloves, minced

1/2 tsp fennel seeds

1 lb. farfalle (bow tie) pasta

Bring a large stockpot of water to a boil. Add pasta and cook according to package directions. During last 3 minutes of cooking, add broccolini.

Meanwhile, heat oil in a sauté pan over medium heat and cook sausages until no pink remains. Remove sausage from pan; add garlic and fennel seeds and cook 1 min till fragrant.

Add sausages back to pan and lower heat. Using a slotted spoon, remove broccolini and pasta and add to sauté pan. Add some pasta water (2 tbsp to 1/4 c.) to make sauce. Sprinkle with red pepper flakes if desired and serve.

Calories 727.2. Total Fat 28.6 g, Sat. Fat 13.2 g, Polyunsat, Fat 4.9 g, Monounsat. Fat 18.8 g. Cholesterol 86.5 mg, Sodium 1042.2 mg, Potassium 263.9 mg, Total Carbs 93.3 g, Dietary Fiber 13.6 g, Sugars 5.4 g, Protein 32.2 g

# Quick Tomato Basil Pasta

Serves 2

20 minute cooking time

Tomato sauce over pasta is one of my favorite easy meals. In summer, I like to make a fresh tomato sauce that takes just a few minutes of cooking and tastes a lot less sugary than the jarred stuff. If you don't want to open a whole can of tomato paste for just a tiny amount, I suggest investing in a tube of tomato paste, usually found on the top shelf in a box in the canned tomato section of your store. It may cost a little bit more than a can, but it can be stored in the fridge for a long time and you won't end up wasting a whole can. As for the red wine, if you don't have a bottle laying around, you can get some red cooking wine that will keep better than an opened bottle of wine.

1/2 lb tomatoes, chopped
2 cloves garlic, minced
1 tsp Italian herb seasoning
1/4 tsp salt
2 tbsp red wine
1 tsp tomato paste
1/2 lb whole wheat linguine
Basil leaves

In a large stockpot, cook pasta according to package directions. Drain, reserving 1 c. of pasta water.

For sauce, heat a large sauté pan over medium heat. Add 1 tbsp olive oil, then cook garlic for 30 seconds. Add tomatoes, spices and tomato paste and cook for 5 minutes. Add wine and cook for a minute more. Add pasta to sauce along with about 1/4 c. pasta water to thin sauce. Stir to combine, then serve with basil leaves sprinkled over the top.

Calories 312.5. Total Fat 8.2 g, Sat. Fat 1.0 g, Polyunsat, Fat 0.7 g, Monounsat. Fat 5.0 g. Cholesterol 0 mg, Sodium 322.5 mg, Potassium 309.2 mg, Total Carbs 49.1 g, Dietary Fiber 6.4 g, Sugars 2.4 g, Protein 8.3 g

# Salmon, Fennel and Kale Pasta

Serves 4

30 minute cook time

For those of you who are a bit more adventurous in the kitchen, give this recipe a try. It's filled with veggies and salmon in a garlic oil that is delicious. If you can't find fennel, or don't like fennel, feel free to skip it. It adds a ton of flavor, but it is sometimes hard to find. Either way, it's a meal that is sure to be a hit.

1 lb salmon fillet

1/2 box whole wheat penne

1 bunch kale

1 fennel bulb, cut in half and sliced

1 clove garlic, minced

1/4 c. white wine

Juice of 1 lemon

1/2 tsp salt

1/4 tsp pepper

Parmesan, grated

Bring a stock pot of water to a boil, then cook penne according to package directions. Drain and set aside.

Heat 1 tbsp olive oil in a large sauté pan over medium-high heat. Season salmon fillet with 1/4 tsp salt and 1/8 tsp pepper, then sear skin side up for 2 minutes. Flip over fillet and cook for 4 minutes, then set aside. Once cool enough to handle, flake fish, removing skin and bones.

Add fennel to sauté pan and sauté for 7 minutes over medium heat until almost soft. Add garlic and kale and sauté for 1 minute. Add lemon juice and wine and 1/4 tsp salt and 1/8 tsp pepper and sauté until kale is wilted. Add flaked salmon to fennel mixture, along with pasta. Stir to mix and serve with grated Parmesan.

Calories 446.3. Total Fat 13.4 g, Sat. Fat 2.5 g, Polyunsat, Fat 3.3 g, Monounsat. Fat 5.7 g. Cholesterol 65.6 mg, Sodium 275.1 mg, Potassium 938.5 mg, Total Carbs 39.7 g, Dietary Fiber 7.0 g, Sugars 2.6 g, Protein 39.7 g

# Rice Bowls

Rice bowls are awesome! They can be so easy to make and as simple as throwing some stuff in a pot and letting it simmer until the rice is done. Others are made by cooking the rice in a rice cooker, then topping with a curry or some steak.

I have also included a great use for leftover rice: fried rice. I make mine with some BBQ Pork and tons of mixed veggies for a quick but satisfying meal. Yum!

# Cilantro Lime Steak with Corn and Rice

Serves 2
20 minute cook time

My boyfriend loves my cilantro lime steak. I'm sure he loves me too but he really loves my cilantro lime steak. So much that it's the most requested meal from him. I usually serve it with some hawed corn kernels and maybe some rice that I've spiced up with a little taco seasoning (about 1/2 tbsp per cup of uncooked rice). It's a perfect date night meal that is classy but comforting.

Two 4 oz steaks, your favorite cut
1 c. corn kernels, thawed
Cooked rice

Cilantro Lime Sauce:
Juice and zest of 1 lime
1/2 bunch green onions, sliced
Handful cilantro
1/4 c. olive oil
1/2 tsp salt
1/4 tsp pepper

Heat a large sauté pan over medium high heat. Sprinkle with salt and pepper, and sear steak, turning once. After steaks are cooked to your liking, set aside and keep warm.

Meanwhile, in a food processor combine lime juice and zest, green onions and cilantro. Process until chopped finely. Add olive oil, salt and pepper and process until emulsified. Pour dressing over steaks and serve with corn and rice.

For steak and corn: Calories 479.1. Total Fat 32.1 g, Sat. Fat 5.3 g, Polyunsat, Fat 2.8 g, Monounsat. Fat 21.8 g. Cholesterol 64.6 mg, Sodium 647.4 mg, Potassium 708.6 mg, Total Carbs 22.1 g, Dietary Fiber 2.9 g, Sugars 3.9 g, Protein 28.7 g

# Asian Salmon and Pea Rice Bowl

Makes 1 bowl

10 minute cook time

I have been making this dish since college, except the difference now is that I use an actual stove instead of a microwave. When I lived in the dorms, I would buy some peas from the salad bar and some pre-cooked rice, then buy a salmon fillet from the store and steam it in my microwave. Now, I like to cook my own rice in a rice cooker and then use thawed peas and sear my salmon in a pan before flaking. The taste is even better now, and just as easy to make.

1/4 lb. salmon fillet
1 c. cooked rice
1/2 c. frozen peas
2 tsp soy sauce
1/4 tsp sesame oil

In a medium sauté pan, heat 1 tsp oil over medium high heat, then add salmon fillet, skin side up, for 2-3 minutes, then flip. Cook salmon on the skin side down for 3-4 more minutes until fillet is cooked through and begins to flake. Set aside to cool.

Cook peas in a small bowl in the microwave for 1 minute. Add to bowl with rice, and cook for another minute. Remove skin from salmon then flake into bite sized pieces. Place on top of the rice and peas, then drizzle with the soy sauce and sesame oil. Serve with a little Sriracha if heat is desired.

Calories 641.9. Total Fat 26.3 g, Sat. Fat 7.5 g, Polyunsat, Fat 7.4 g, Monounsat. Fat 11 g. Cholesterol 113.3 mg, Sodium 1303.6 mg, Potassium 994.1 mg, Total Carbs 46.1 g, Dietary Fiber 0.8 g, Sugars 0.5 g, Protein 50.8 g

# Mexican Beans and Rice

Serves 4

30 minute cook time

I love beans and rice. They go so well together, especially when they can be cooked in one pot together. This dish was one of my first rice and bean creations. I wanted something like Spanish rice with tomatoes and a smoky, Mexican seasoning. If you want a little extra added to it, feel free to add some thawed frozen corn, or maybe some diced pickled jalapenos, or even some cilantro. Any of those are delicious.

1 c. rice
1/2 yellow onion, diced
1 clove garlic, minced
14 oz. can diced tomatoes with juices
1 tbsp taco seasoning
1 tsp tomato paste
1 3/4 c. water
14 oz can black beans, drained and rinsed
1 avocado, sliced

In a medium saucepan, heat 1 tbsp oil over medium heat. Add onions and garlic and sauté for 2-3 minutes until onions begin to soften. Add rice and stir for 1minute to coat in oil. Add tomatoes, seasoning, tomato paste and water. Bring to a boil, then reduce to a simmer and cook for 12 minutes. Add beans and cook for another minute to heat beans through. Serve with avocado and some hot sauce.

Calories 272. Total Fat 6.3 g, Sat. Fat 0.5 g, Polyunsat, Fat 0.3 g, Monounsat. Fat 2.6 g. Cholesterol 0 mg, Sodium 335.9 mg, Potassium 533.5 mg, Total Carbs 49.0 g, Dietary Fiber 6.4 g, Sugars 1.7 g, Protein 9.0 g

# Curried Salmon over Rice

Serves 4

30 minutes cooking time

I know, I know this book is supposed to be filled with recipes meant for only 1 or 2 people, so why do I have one that is for 4? Because it is so easy to make and so good that you will want to have leftovers! And it is so customizable. If you don't want salmon, try chunks of chicken or if you want a vegetarian versions, you can leave the meat out. You can also choose which vegetables you want. I like bell peppers, onions and carrots, but feel free to add peas or sweet potatoes or green beans. All are welcome in this dish. But beware, when you are at the store, read the label of the curry paste! I had to search to find a mild one; the rest were on the super spicy side!

1/2 lb salmon fillet, skin on
1 red bell pepper, cut into chunks
1/2 yellow onion, sliced
1 c. baby carrots, each carrot cut into thirds
2-3 tbsp of green curry paste (found in the Asian section of your store)
14 oz can of coconut milk (full fat please!)
Thai basil leaves, if desired
Cooked rice, to serve

In a large sauté pan, heat 1 tbsp oil over medium high heat. Cook salmon fillet skin side down for 1 minute, leaving most of the salmon raw. Remove salmon from heat and let cool, then remove the skin. Cut into 1" cubes and set aside.

Clean out any scales from the pan, then add another 1 tbsp of oil. Reduce heat to medium. Add curry paste and sauté for 3 minutes until fragrant. Add veggies and salmon and cook for 2 minutes, stirring to coat everything in curry paste. Add coconut milk, then let simmer for 15 minutes until salmon is cooked and sauce has thickened. Serve hot over rice.

Without rice: Calories 172.3. Total Fat 8.2 g, Sat. Fat 4.0 g, Polyunsat, Fat 1.9 g, Monounsat. Fat 3.4 g. Cholesterol 28.3 mg, Sodium 456.7 mg, Potassium 303.5 mg, Total Carbs 13.5 g, Dietary Fiber 2.1 g, Sugars 7.6 g, Protein 12.8 g

# "Fried" Rice

Serves 2
15 minute cooking time

Fried rice is a great way to use up leftover rice, especially if you go light on the oil and add lots of veggies. Be sure to add in the Chinese five spice! It gives it a more restaurant-y taste that is absolutely divine.

1 c. leftover rice
1/4 lb BBQ Pork, chopped into small pieces
1 c. frozen mixed veggies, thawed
1/2 yellow onion, chopped
1 clove garlic, minced
1/4 c. soy sauce
2 tbsp mirin (rice wine) or white wine
1 tbsp sesame oil
1/4 tsp Chinese five spice

In a small bowl, combine soy sauce, mirin, sesame oil and Chinese five spice. Set aside. Heat a large skillet over medium high heat. Add onions and garlic and sauté until onion is translucent, about 2-3 minutes. Add veggies and sauce mixture and stir fry for 1 minute. Add rice and cook, continually stirring and breaking up chunks of rice until mixture is heated through and all the grains of rice are coated in sauce. Add BBQ pork and stir to mix. Serve hot.

Calories 379.7. Total Fat 10.2 g, Sat. Fat 1.8 g, Polyunsat, Fat 3.2 g, Monounsat. Fat 2.8 g. Cholesterol 36.7 mg, Sodium 2518.9 mg, Potassium 328.5 mg, Total Carbs 53.3 g, Dietary Fiber 5.3 g, Sugars 5.9 g, Protein 21.4 g

# Index

The nutritional information provided at the bottom of each page is for the exact recipe, but will vary depending on brand of ingredients and accuracy of measurements.

.

# About the author

Hello! I'm so glad you picked up my third cookbook. I have so thoroughly enjoyed writing this book about easy and quick recipes.

A little bit about me then eh? I have been cooking since I could walk, helping my grandma bake cookies or make dumplings. I even did some experimenting without a recipe and ended up with salty hockey pucks, as my grandpa will attest to being force fed several. In addition to doing chemistry in the kitchen, I have had food allergies almost my whole life, and have been dairy and egg free since 2011, which has made my culinary adventure even more exciting.

Outside of the kitchen, I have been skiing since before I was 2, and I still love it. A new love of mine that has cropped up in the past few years is hiking. Growing up in the Puget Sound area has definitely influenced my cooking style, and I plan to stay put. I am working on many more cookbooks, so keep your eyes open for much more.

Made in the USA
San Bernardino, CA
21 February 2017